Book 2 Easy Intermediate

Three's A Crowd

These trios can be performed with any other combination of instruments within Book 2.

Violin

A mix and match collection of 19 trio arrangements by James Power.

CHESTER MUSIC
London/New York/Paris/Sydney/Copenhagen/Berlin/Madrid/Tokyo

Contents

Published by
Chester Music
14-15 Berners Street, London W1T 3LJ, UK.

Exclusive Distributors:

Music Sales Limited
Distribution Centre, Newmarket Road, Bury St Edmunds, Suffolk IP33 3YB, England,

Music Sales Corporation
257 Park Avenue South, New York, NY 10010, United States of America.

Music Sales Pty Limited
20 Resolution Drive, Caringbah, NSW 2229, Australia.

Order No. PM234626R
ISBN 0-7119-9380-7

The instruments featured on the cover were provided by Macari's Musical Instruments, London.
Models provided by Truly Scrumptious and Norrie Carr.
Photography by George Taylor.
Printed in the United Kingdom.

Greensleeves

Traditional English

Grandfather's Clock

Traditional

C
Vln 1
Vln 2
Vln 3
f
(f)
To CODA
D
mf
D.S. al CODA
CODA
rit.
mp
pizz.
arco
(mf)

The Entertainer

Scott Joplin (1868-1917)

Fine
B
17
22
27
32
Vln 1
Vln 2
Vln 3
cresc.
D.S. al Fine

The Yellow Rose Of Texas

Traditional American

C
26
Vln 1
Vln 2
Vln 3
D
33
f
E
40
mf
46
f

Für Elise

Ludwig van Beethoven (1770-1827)

Allegro

Wolfgang Amadeus Mozart (1756-1791)

The Big Brass Band

James Power

Melody
Vln 1
Vln 2
Vln 3
B
To CODA
D.S. al CODA
Solo
CODA

A French Frolic

Traditional

B
22
Vln 1
Vln 2
Vln 3
To CODA
C
27
f
mp
Melody
ff
D.S. al CODA
1.
2.
33
mf
CODA
39
Opt.
ff

O Come All Ye Faithful

Traditional Christmas Song

Ding Dong Merrily On High

Traditional Christmas Song

Ecossaise

Ludwig van Beethoven (1770-1827)

Buffalo Gals

Traditional American

Rag Doll

James Power

18
Vln 1
Vln 2
Vln 3
C
23
Vln 1
Vln 2
Vln 3
To CODA
D.S. al CODA
28
Vln 1
Vln 2
Vln 3
CODA
32
Vln 1
Vln 2
Vln 3

Bill Bailey

Traditional American

C
21
Vln 1
Vln 2
Vln 3
mf
f
D
27
p
33
1.
2.
cresc.
39
ff

Traditional Tunes Of Scotland

Traditional

Fine
Vln 1
Vln 2
Vln 3
D
L'istesso Tempo
E
D.S. al Fine
1.
2.

Radetsky March

Johann Strauss I (1804-1849)

Fine
C
18
Vln 1
Vln 2
Vln 3
f
22
D
27
D.S. al Fine
33
dim.

Minuet

Wolfgang Amadeus Mozart (1756-1791)

18
1.
2.
Vln 1
Vln 2
Vln 3
mf
p
C
23
f
27
mp
31
cresc.

Dance Of The Little Swans

Pyotr Ilyich Tchaikovsky (1840-1893)

15
1.
Vln 1
Vln 2
Vln 3
18
2.
C
mp
mp
mp
22
1.
2.
cresc. poco a poco
cresc. poco a poco
cresc. poco a poco
25
ff
ff
ff

Pyramids

Timing and tuning exercise